Tillie & Clementine & Mikey

By Dan Killeen

Happy Fun Books
St. Louis

Published by
Happy Fun Books
St. Louis, MO

Please visit
HappyFunBooks.com

ISBN 978-0-9898474-7-6

Printed in Canada

For Mikey

There once was a girl named Tillie, and she had a sister named Clementine, and they loved to have fun.

4

Tillie and Clementine weren't so sure this was great news. At school the next day, their friends had much to say about the idea.

7

8

9

10

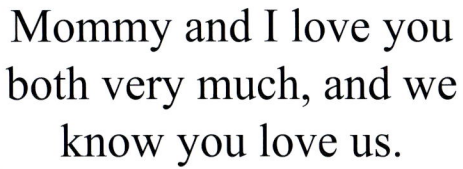

11

15

That night, Clementine fell asleep happy that their family would soon grow by one. Tillie, though, lay awake for a while still worrying about how their lives were going to change.

16

Meanwhile, a phone call came in from Ms. Betty at the adoption agency.

That night, Mommy and Daddy spoke with a very brave, loving mommy who was looking for a good family to adopt her newborn baby boy.

Later that week, Mommy and Daddy boarded a plane at the busy airport.

Back home Nana, Pop, and the girls began preparing the place for Mikey.

21

In Brotherlove City
the two families met
in person and talked
for a good long while.

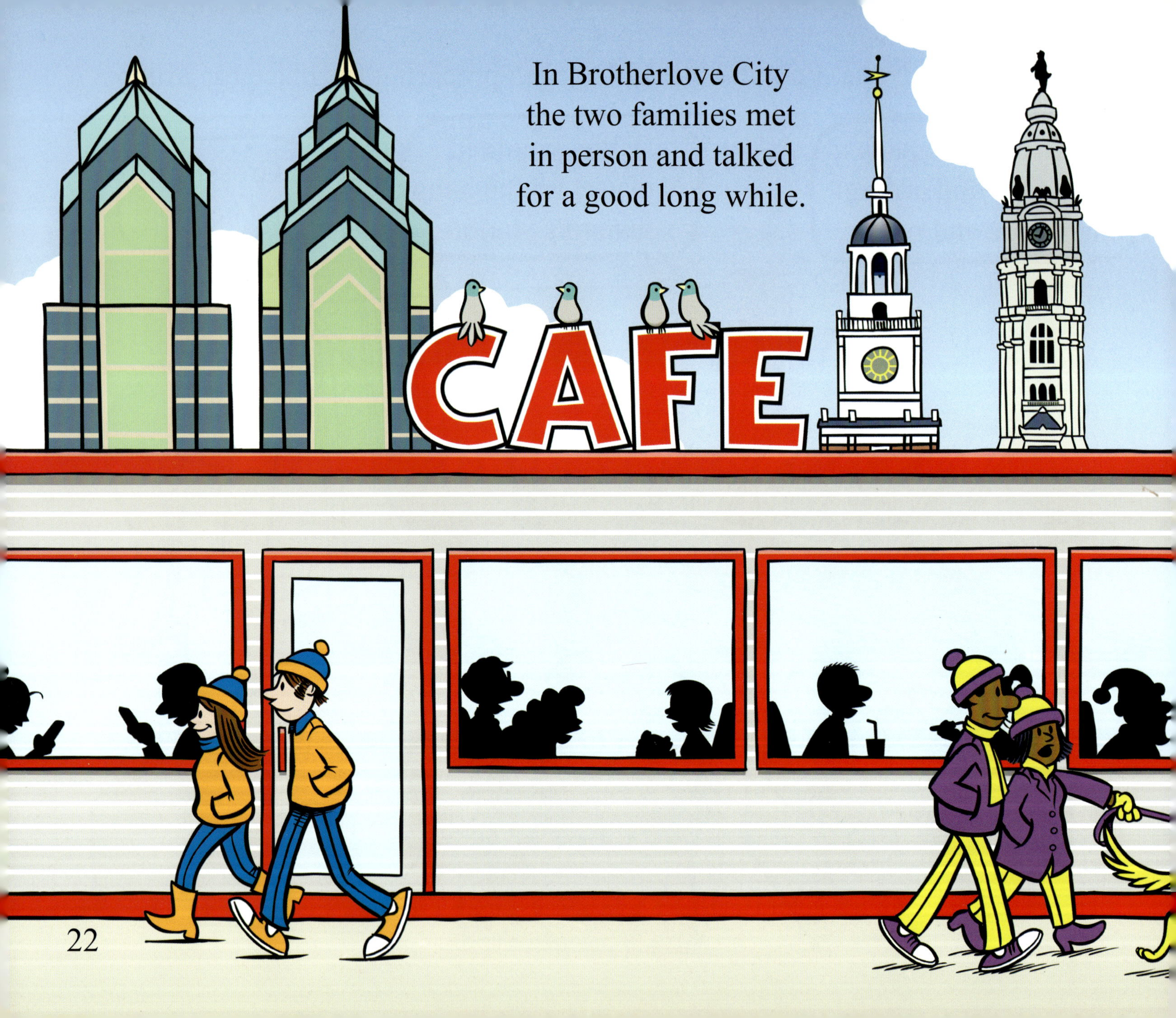

Mikey was there too, being held by
his new parents for the first time.

Over the next few days Mikey got to know Mommy and Daddy while the folks of Brotherlove City cheered him on.

Hi, Mom! We're flying home tomorrow. How are things back there?

On the trip back to Rivertown, the whole flight crew was happy for Mikey as he was about to meet his new sisters and see his new home.

Tillie, though, still had doubts as she arrived at the airport with her grandparents and Clementine.

27

Tillie and Clementine walked into the airport to find their aunts, uncles, and cousins already there, ready to welcome the newest member of the family.

28

29

All of Tillie's questions, doubts, and worries
quickly vanished as she held her new baby brother.

31

With Mikey now part of the family, everything seemed better. Dinner was yummier.

Carpool was more fun.

33

And Daddy's bedtime
stories were more exciting.

And they also didn't mind that Mikey
was a boy and sometimes loud.

RAWR!

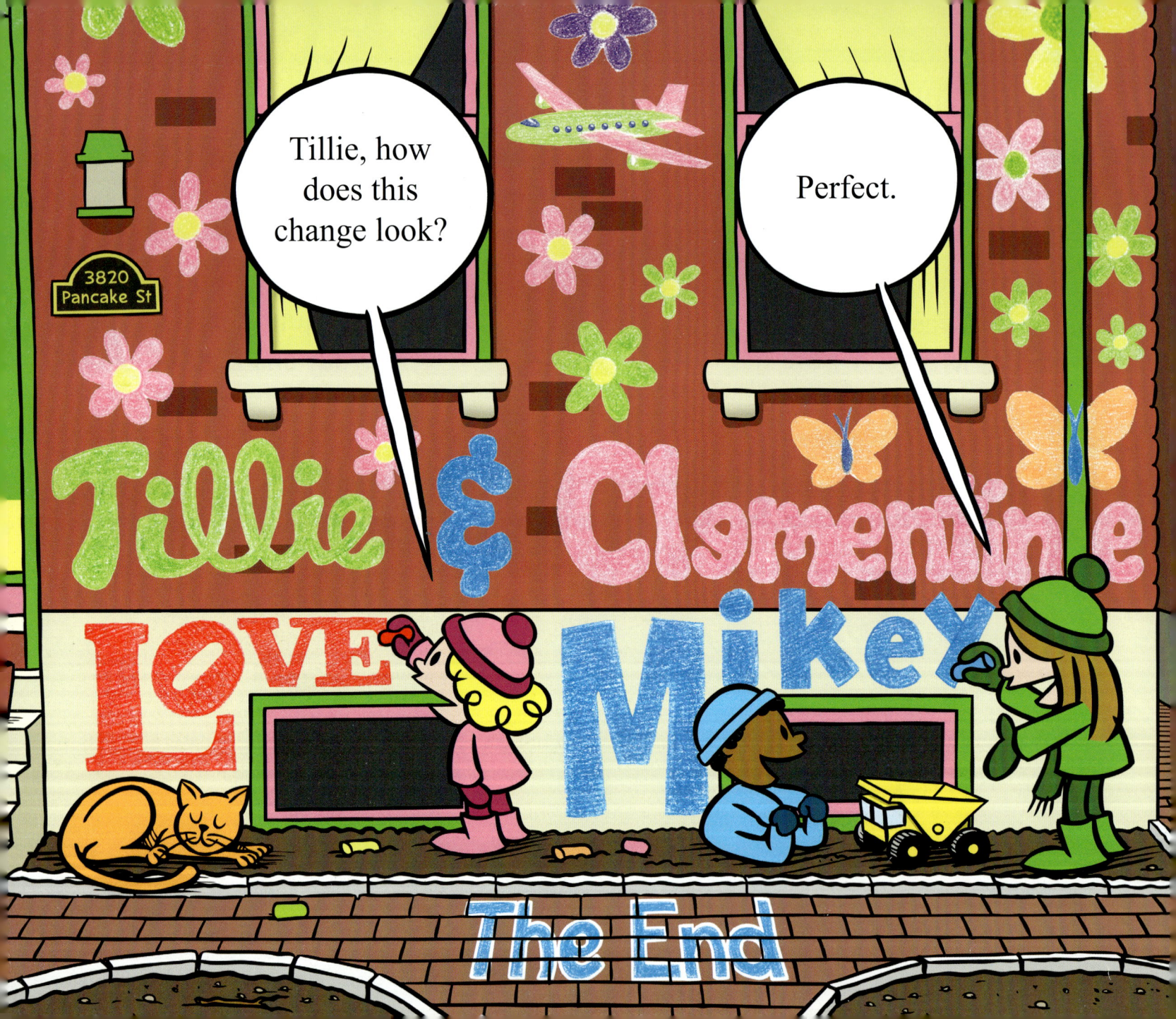